INDIAN IMMIGRANTS IN UNITED KINGDOM

About the Author

Dr. K.S. Dhindsa is a Professor of Economics at the Punjab School of Economics, Guru Nanak Dev University, Amritsar (India). Dr. Dhindsa has a brilliant career, who after graduating from Punjab University, completed the post-graduate diploma in Economic Development from Glasgow University. Thereafter, he obtained his Master Degree from Leeds University (England). Then he went to London University where he successfully completed his Ph.D. degree. He has published a book titled "India's Export Performance–Some Policy Implications". He has published a fairly large number of research papers in National and International journals. For his post-doctorate he went to the School of Oriental and African Studies, University of London, during 1989-91. He was the Editor of *Indian Journal of Quantitative Economics*–A Journal of international Development, during 1994-96. He was the Dean of Faculty of Economics & Business during 1992-93 and was Chairman of Punjab School of Economics, during 1994-96.

INDIAN IMMIGRANTS IN UNITED KINGDOM

A SOCIO-ECONOMIC ANALYSIS

K.S. DHINDSA

CONCEPT PUBLISHING COMPANY, NEW DELHI - 110059

ISBN 81-7022-728-3

First Published 1998

Published and Printed by
Ashok Kumar Mittal
Concept Publishing Company
A/15-16, Commercial Block, Mohan Garden,
NEW DELHI - 110059
Phone: 5648039, 5649024
Fax : 091-(11)-5648053

DEDICATED

TO

MY BELOVED PARENTS

PREFACE

In many advanced countries of the world like Europe, Japan and U.S.A., the share of population above sixty-five years has increased, while the share of younger working population has declined. In order to meet the shortage of working population in these countries, the migration of labourers from labour-surplus less developed countries to these advanced countries cannot be avoided in the near future. Many empirical studies point out that increasing supply of immigrants may have little impact on the wages of the workers in the host country. The impact of immigrants on growth of host countries also depends on the skill level of these immigrants. The immigration surplus will remain positive so long as unskilled and skilled flow of workers reduce the wages of both these types of workers respectively in the host country. The impact of emigration on the labour-exporting countries will be favourable, if the remittances sent by these workers are being used for investment purposes rather than consumption purposes. Emigrants' remittances not only provide much needed foreign exchange but also provide additional capital which is desperately needed by capital scarce economies like India. Keeping this in view the importance of remittances for Indian economy, the Indian government at all levels—national, state, and local—is developing programmes to encourage investment by the non-resident Indians.

In the present study an attempt has been made to study various issues relating to labour migration from India to United Kingdom. The specific issues discussed in the study are like the causes of emigration from Indian Punjab to U.K., the educational and skill level of migrants, their awareness regarding various schemes for attracting foreign remittances, total amount of remittances sent home by the migrants and their uses in the place of their origin. When people migrate from India to U.K., they find themselves in a completely different culture and that is why they take some time to settle down and assimilate the culture of the foreign country. So the study also discusses the assimilation problems of Indian migrants and the retainment of Indian cultural values by the children of these people abroad.

The survey of the present study was conducted in U.K. For this purpose a sample of 540 migrants settled in U.K., was taken by using the multi-stage random sampling technique. All these migrants belong to different tehsils/towns of three districts of Punjab, namely Jalandhar, Kapurthala and Hoshiarpur, from where the majority of people migrated.

Though some studies on labour migration pertaining to states like Kerala, Gujarat and Punjab are available but none of them covers all the aspects regarding labour migration to foreign countries. This study has therefore been undertaken to analyse systematically various socio-economic issues regarding labour migration. This study would be very much useful for the students of Economics in India as well as abroad. This study can also be useful for Race Relation Boards, Labour Bureau, Foreign Investment Promotion Board and Immigration Departments particularly for the formulation of immigration policies.

The study has been divided into five chapters. The introductory chapter deals with the theoretical aspects of immigration like the impact of immigrants on wages, employment and growth of the host country and the impact of immigration on sending countries. The second chapter presents the research design, data source and methodology used in the study. Alongwith it some theoretical framework regarding the mode of utilisation of remittances in the home country has also been presented. The other two chapters in succession analyse empirical by the socio-economic characteristics of he immigrants settled in U.K., the amount of remittances and their utilisation in the home country, assimilation problems faced by these immigrants and the retainment of Indian cultural values by these people in U.K. Besides it, the views of the children of these immigrants regarding love/arranged marriages have also been discussed. The final chapter presents the summary, conclusion and policy implications of the study.

K.S. DHINDSA,
Professor,
Punjab School of Economics,
Guru Nanak Dev University,
Amritsar (Punjab)
India

CONTENTS

ACKNOWLEDGEMENTS

This research was carried out when the author was a Post-Doctoral Fellow at the School of Oriental and African Studies, during 1990-91.

The author is highly indebted to Professor Graham P. Chapman, SOAS, University of London, who gave ample encouragement during the whole tenure of the research project. He was kind enough to give time. The author is also grateful to the staff member of SOAS, who gave useful comments at the seminar held on this project. Thanks are also due to staff members of Economics Department of the London School of Economics (LSE) with whom the author had discussions about this project. Also, the author is grateful to Guru Nanak Dev University for granting study leave to undertake this Post-Doctoral Research.

K.S. DHINDSA

1

INTRODUCTION

Internal migration from one region to another region usually takes place due to regional wage differentials. Similarly due to intra-country wage differentials, people migrate from low wage to high wage countries. South-North migration is also caused by demographic differences in age structure and fertility. Younger people from many southern countries migrate to countries that have lower fertility rates and ageing population. The labour shortages experienced in many European countries during the 1950s and 1960s made some European countries like the United Kingdom to adopt a liberal immigration policy. Taking advantage of this policy, many people migrated from South Asian countries to United Kingdom. France also received a large number of immigrants from its colonies in Africa. However, these very countries transformed their policy into a restricted one after the oil crisis of the 1970s and the recessionary fears it generated. Unemployment was expected to rise to alarming levels, and consequently it became necessary to counter the threat of further increases in unemployment figures carried by immigrants. But such restrictive immigration policies will have to be relaxed in the future because of a sharp decline in the working population.

In Europe, Japan and United States, the share of population over 65 years has increased[1], while the share of younger working population has decreased. Therefore, migration from South to North is unavoidable in the near future.

Impact of Immigrants on Wages, Employment and Growth in the Host/ Receiving Country

It is feared that immigration will lower wages or make large number of domestic workers unemployed. In the face of high substitutability of foreign for domestic workers and since immigrants are willing to accept lower wage levels, immigration could cause a decline in native workers' wages. But if institutional factors like strong trade unions successfully oppose hiring of workers at lower wages and thereby maintain rigid wage structures as is the case in European countries, then immigration would result in higher unemployment. At the same time, trade unions may try to set wage level higher than equilibrium wage rates[2] and this in turn would lead to unemployment among unskilled workers.

Theoretically, the impact of immigrants on native factors of production like labour and capital will depend upon the degree of substitutability between immigrants and natives and on the fact whether the host economy is closed or open to international trade. In a closed economy model, immigrants will increase the price of factors of production with which they are complementary, decrease the price of factors with which they are perfect substitutes and have an ambiguous effect on the price of factors with which they are imperfect substitutes.

Take the example of country where unskilled labour can be substituted for capital and skilled labour, while the two latter factors of production are complementary to each other. Immigration of skilled workers will lower the wages of skilled workers. A rise in employment of skilled people will cause increase in the demand for complementary factor, capital. Hence the return to capital will increase. On the other hand, immigration of unskilled workers will lower the wages of unskilled workers. (The impact of unskilled immigrants on capital and skilled workers will be vague). Immigration may lower the wages more if immigrants are prepared to work at wage rates lower than natives. This seems possible if the immigrants do not know the host country's language and if high unemployment exists in the host country. Employers often give lower wages to illegal immigrants which the latter readily accept. Thus an influx of such immigrants shifts labour supply and makes it more elastic.

Let us now take the case of an open economy model in which factor endowments are not too different across countries. Trade will be caused due to difference in factor endowments and factor price equalization will occur. Immigration of unskilled labour will make the host country produce and export more of labour intensive goods. On the other hand, if factor endowments are quite different across countries, then countries, instead of producing all goods, will tend to specialise in goods requiring more of relatively abundant factor. In such a situation, the impact of immigrants will have effects similar to those of closed economy. Thus, an influx of immigrants increase the size of labour force which allows firms to lower wages and raise employment. If the wage is made more rigid due to institutional arrangement, then unemployment could rise. This raises the question as to whether the rise in unemployment among natives and immigrants would be evenly distributed. It seems more probable that unemployment would rise more among immigrants than natives.

But this issue needs to be studied empirically. However, it is quite likely that due to the fall in unskilled wage caused by migration of unskilled workers, some natives may leave jobs or reduce their hours of work and thus the employment rate of natives may fall.

Many empirical studies have been conducted to examine the impact of immigration on wages and employment.[3] The correlation between mean wage and salary income of large metropolitan cities in the U.S.A. and the fraction of foreign born population has been found to be high and positive.[4] This suggests that immigrants do not have an adverse impact on the host country's wage rate. An absence of reduction in wage structure may be observed when less migration of natives occurs to those cities having a higher fraction of immigrant population.[5] While summing up the impact of immigrants on native wages, it can be concluded that immigrants may negligibly lower native wages. For instance, every ten percent rise of immigrant population, native wage is reduced by one percent.

Impact of Immigration on Growth

With the help of Solow's growth model[6], the impact of immigration on growth can be examined. In this model, production is considered to be a function of labour, capital and human capital. In the absence of trade between countries, a country receives immigrants if it has a high physical capital/labour ratio which implies a higher wage rate. It is assumed that immigrants bring human capital but not physical capital with them. In such a model, the impact of immigration depends on whether immigrants bring human capital sufficient to offset the dilution of physical capital per person due to influx of immigrants in the receiving country. If immigrants possess more human capital than natives, then pace of growth will be faster[7]. On the other hand, if the level of immigrants human capital is lower than that of natives, the pace of growth will be lower. Thus for studying the impact of immigrants on growth, it is crucial to know the level of human capital immigrants carry as compared to that of the natives. Empirical studies show that immigrants to Organisation for Economic Corporation and Development (OECD) have lower human capital than natives.[8]

Immigration Surplus

Ignoring the role of capital in the production process, immigration surplus[9] is to be positive if the skill composition of immigrants differs from that of natives. If the skill composition of immigrants were the same as of natives, the constant returns to scale production implies that factor price or wages of skilled and unskilled workers remain unaffected by immigration, and hence native workers have nothing to gain from immigration. Thus native workers will gain from immigration if the skill composition of immigrants is different than that of the natives.

When we bring in the role of capital stock in the production process, immigration surplus will depend on the elasticity of factor price for skilled and unskilled workers. If the elasticity of factor price is larger for skilled workers than for unskilled workers, then the immigration surplus will be greater. This implies that wages of skilled workers are more responsive to a shift in skilled labour supply than the wages of unskilled workers. The skilled immigrant flow generates surplus because of relatively high complementarity between capital and skilled labour. However it needs to be pointed out here that immigration surplus is going to be positive so long as unskilled flow reduces wages of unskilled, and skilled immigrants reduce wages of skilled workers. On the basis of efficiency considerations, the objective of the government should be to maximise national income of natives, and this can be achieved by maximising immigration surplus net of the fiscal burden imposed by immigrants on native tax payers. For determining the optimum rise and skill composition of the immigrant flow, one needs to equate the increase in immigration surplus resulting from admitting one more immigrant to the marginal cost of the immigrant.

Viewing from demand side, immigration policy that grants visas only to skilled workers can help maximising immigration surplus. Working from the supply side if the skilled workers are not or less willing to move and unskilled workers more willing to move, then the immigration policy of only admitting skilled workers will cut off the flow. So while framing the immigration policy, the government may have to take into account, apart from social, political and humanitarian considerations, demand and supply side of perspective immigrants.

Impact of Immigration on the Sending Countries

Immigrants send foreign remittances to the countries of their origin and in turn increase effective demand in the sending countries. But if foreign exchange is purchased in the parallel/black market, then domestic supply of goods cannot be increased through import of goods and raw material and this may cause inflationary pressure in the economy. Further, if the local currency—obtained through the exchange of foreign currency in the parallel market—is used for consumption and not for investment, then domestic supply of goods cannot be increased and thereby causing inflationary pressure in the economy. If, on the other hand, foreign remittances come through official channel, then the foreign remittances received in foreign currency by banks can be used for importing goods and raw materials, thus causing no inflationary pressure in the economy. Further, if domestic currency—obtained in exchange for foreign currency from the parallel market—is used for investment rather than consumption, then domestic supply of goods can be increased and thus foreign remittances may help reduce inflation rate.

Migration through remittances is likely to accelerate capital formation and technical change on small peasant farms. Since the people with low income migrate, remittances sent by them to native villages/cities will redistribute income in their favour, thus narrowing down income differentials. If, on the other hand, the income from remittances is used for non-productive expenditure, then remittances will not improve distribution of income, and this will simply reinforce the dependence of the native people upon immigrants.

Benefits of Immigration to the Host Countries

Immigration is beneficial to the host countries.[10]

First, immigrants expand the size of the market through an increase in the effective demand for goods and services. Secondly, immigration may make labour markets work more effectively. This is possible because immigrants increase labour supply and thus they help eroding institutional constraints—e.g. weakening workers' unions/trade unions. Thirdly, immigrants provide different goods in the service sector. Fourthly, immigrants increase native productivity because the unskilled labour inputs of immigrants are often complementary to that of the skilled labour of native workers in production. Further, productivity may rise because domestic firms may pick up free knowledge as a result of new interactions among immigrant workers and firms.

Finally immigration also redistributes income from native workers who compete with immigrants, to capitalist class. Because of relatively high marginal propensity to save of the capitalists, saving and investment will be greater and this in turn will cause substantial increase in national income of the receiving countries through multiplier effect.

NOTES AND REFERENCES

1. For details about age structure in Japan, USA and European Union countries, see OECD, *"Aging Population: The Social Policy Implications,"* 1988.
2. See, Earl Shapiro and Joseph Stiglitz, "Equilibrium unemployment as a Discipline Device," *American Economic Review,* June 1984, Vol. 74.
3. See, for example studies given below:

J. Altonji and D. Card, "The Effects of Immigration on the Labour Market Outcomes of Less Skilled Natives in edited book by J. Abowd and R. Freeman, *Trade and The Labour Market,* Chicago University Press, 1991, pp. 2002-2034.

R. Lalonde and R. Topel, "Labour Market Adjustments to increased Immigration" in J. Abowd and R. Freeman (eds.) *Immigration Trade and The Labour Market,* Chicago University Press 1991. pp. 167-200.

C. Goldin, "The Political Economy of Immigration Restriction in the United States, 1890-1921," in C. Goldin and G. Libecap (eds.) *The Regulated Economy: A Historical Approach to Political Economy,* Chicago University Press, 1994, pp. 223-257.

G. Borjas, R. Freeman and K. Lang, "Undocumented Mexican - Born Workers in the United States: How many? How Permanent? in J. Abowd and R. Freeman (eds.) *Immigration, Trade and the Labour Market,* University of Chicago Press, 1991, pp. 77-100.

Borjas and Ramey study suggests that one percentage point increase in fraction of foreign born population reduces the wage of (native) high school drop-outs relative to college graduates by 0.6 per cent.

For details see:

G. Borjas and V. Ramey, "Foreign competition, Market Power and Wage Inequality: Theory and Evidence" National Bureau of Economic Research (NBER) *Working Paper* 4556, 1993.

Pope and Withers find no negative effects of immigration on Australian Natives over the period 1961-1981.

For details, see D. Pope and G. Withers: "Do migrants rob jobs? Lessons of the Australian History 1861-1991" *Journal of Economic History,* December 1993, Vol. 53, pp. 719-42.

Pischke and Velling find no significant detrimental effect of immigrants on employment/unemployment.

For details see Jorn-Steffen Pischke and Johannes Velling, "Wage and Employment Effects of Immigration to Germany: An Analysis Based on

Local Markets," *Working Paper,* MIT, 1994.

4. The correlation coefficient is found to be 0.58. Calculated from data obtained from US Bureau of the Census, General, Social and Economic characteristics, 1990 Census of Population Washington DC.
5. The following studies show that internal migrants in the United States avoided those areas where immigrants were arriving from abroad.

   For details, see:

   R. Filer, "The Impact of Immigrant Arrivals on Migratory Patterns of Native Workers in edited work by G. Borjas and R. Freeman, *Immigration and the Work Force: Economic Consequences for the United States and Source Areas,* Chicago University Press, 1992, pp. 245-70.

   M. White and Z. Liang, "The Effect of Immigration on the Internal Migration of Native Born Population, 1981-90, mimeo, Brown University, 1994.

   M. White and L. Hunter, "The Migratory Response of Native-Born Workers to the Presence of Immigrants in the Labour Market" Brown University PSTC *Working Paper 93-08,* July 1993.
6. See Robert Solow, "A Contribution to the Theory of Economic Growth," *Quarterly Journal of Economics,* February 1956, Vol. 70, pp. 65-94.
7. These models assume physical capital to be immobile and labour and human capital to be mobile across countries.
8. J. Dolado, A. Goria and A. Ichino, "Immigration, Human capital and Growth in the Host Country", *Working Paper* Fomdazione ENI, Enrico Mattei 1993.
9. An Immigration surplus arises when native wages fall as a result of immigration. Although native workers get low wage rate, these losses are more than offset by the increase in income accruing to capitalists, through a higher rental price of capital.
10. For knowing details about economic benefits from immigration to the host country, see the theoretical model given by Bhagwati and Srinivasan.

    Jagdish N. Bhagwati and T.N. Srinivasan, *Lectures on International Trade,* Cambridge, Mass: MIT Press, 1983.

    Also see, George J. Borjas, "The Economics of Immigration," *Journal of Economic Literature,* December 1994, Vol. 32, pp. 1667-717.

    For empirical Analysis of gains from Immigration see, for example. Shirley Svorny, "Consumer Gains from Physician Immigration to the US 1966-1971. *Applied Economics,* February 1991, 23, pp. 331-37.

2

MODE OF UTILISATION OF REMITTANCES

Theoretical Approach

Emigration is not a recent phenomenon in India. During the nineteenth and the early twentieth centuries, the British used to recruit people with a low qualification background to work in other colonies like South Africa, Singapore, Malaysia and Mauritius, etc. After the outbreak of the First World War, emigration dropped significantly. Therefore, emigration continued on a much smaller scale till the period of the Great Depression when it touched its bottom trough. There was intensive emigration during the brief spell of the Second World War period. The process of emigration almost came to its end with the end of British rule in the late 1940s.[1]

The revival of emigration began in the post-independent period, during the late 1950s. Though some people from Punjab came to the UK even before 1950, but the process of emigration in large numbers only started in the late 1950s. Initially, a majority of immigrants were from the poor uppercaste category with relatively small holdings of land. Emigration from Punjab reached its peak during the early 1960s, when the threat of British immigration restrictions encouraged parents, wives, children, relatives and friends to make a hasty move to reach England before the strict immigration control came into force. The process of emigration continued, though on a smaller scale until the 1980s when it became minimal.

The matter of emigrants' remittances sent home, their magnitude and the ways in which they are used is becoming increasingly significant for labour exporting countries like India. Emigrants' remittances not only provide foreign exchange but also additional capital which is desperately needed by capital-scarce economies like

India. Keeping in view the importance of foreign remittances for the Indian economy, the Indian government at all levels — national, state and local—is developing programmes to encourage investment by people of Indian origin living abroad.

Though some studies on emigrants and their remittances pertaining to states like Kerala and Gujarat are available[2], there are few systematic studies regarding emigrants' remittances[3], their utilization, causes of emigration, the emigrants' job status and the assimilation problems of Punjabi immigrants in the UK etc.. This study of Punjabi immigrants in the UK has, therefore, been undertaken to fill up this gap.

Data Base and Methodology

Before coming to UK to undertake this study, a sample of 600 male immigrants to the UK was taken by using the multi-stage random sampling technique. First of all, with the help of travel agencies located in different tehsils/towns of three district of Doaba region, namely Jalandhar, Kapurthala and Hoshiarpur, all the villages — from where the majority of the people emigrated to the UK — were listed. Then one village from each of the four tehsils of every three districts were randomly selected. Thereafter, fifty male emigrants from each of the twelve chosen villages were randomly selected. Thus a representative sample of 600 male emigrants to the UK from the Doaba region of Punjab were selected.

The addresses and telephone numbers of 600 selected immigrants[4] living in the U.K. were taken from their friends and relatives living in Punjab. From their UK addresses it became obvious that these emigrants had settled in different parts of the UK. A large number of immigrants had settled in Birmingham, Sheffield, Bedford, Leeds, Bradford and Luton. Some had settled in towns like Southhall, Hounslow, Cranford, Hays, Harrow (Middlesex), Slough, Reading (Berks), Ilford, Barking, Seven Kings (Essex), Gravesend, Grays, Gillingham, Strood, Chatham (Kent), Crawley (Sussex), Redhill, Horley (Surrey), New Port and Glasgow. Distribution of sampled Punjabi immigrants living in different cities/towns are given in the map. Due to non-availability or changes of addresses, sixty immigrants could not be contacted. This information was obtained only from a sample of 540 immigrants.

It is worth noting that a number of immigrants settled in industrial centres where there was ample employment opportunities during the 1960s. It should also be mentioned here that Punjabi immigrants are fairly scattered, while the majority of Muslim immigrants from Pakistan and Gujrati immigrants from East Africa and India are settled in cities like Bradford and Leicester respectively.

Before drafting the questionnaire in the final form, preliminary interviews were held with some immigrants from whom questions were asked about various aspects regarding this research project. Then after drafting the questionnaire, people living in different parts of UK were contacted through personal visits. Before visiting them, appointments were made on the telephone. In some cases, more than one visit was made to get answers for various questions asked in the questionnaire.

As regards methodology, tabular analysis is done. Various tables have been compiled from the vast data generated through the questionnaire. (See Questionnaire in Appendix).

Theoretical Approach

For analysing the impact of foreign remittances on the sending country, it is essential to estimate the total quantum of remittances sent by non-resident Indians. It will be appropriate here to discuss the macro framework[5] for measuring the amount of foreign remittances sent by immigrants.

Value of total remittances in Indian rupees is equal to total migrants' income abroad (Y_t) minus migrants' consumption abroad (CA_t) converted to Indian rupees at the average effective exchange rate O. Thus:

$$RT_t = O\,(Y_t - CA_t - SA_t)$$

Where RT_c = total remittances in Indian rupees.

Y_t = migrants' income abroad,

CA_t = migrants' consumption abroad.

SA_t = migrants' saving held abroad.

O = average effective exchange rate.

Total migrants' income in foreign currency is equal to total number of migrants (L_t) multiplied by average earnings abroad per worker in foreign currency (W_t). Hence

$$Y_t = W_t . L_t$$

Unrecorded remittances (R_t) are found by subtracting recorded remittances (T_t) from total remittances (RT_t).

$$RT_t - T_t = R_t$$

Unrecorded capital exports expressed in U.S. dollars (K_t) are given by the total value of unrecorded remittances (R_t) minus the unrecorded remittances used for smuggled imports (M_t) and unrecorded factor payments abroad (F_t) converted to $US at the average annual effective exchange rate (O_t).

$$K_t = [R_t - (M_t + .F_t)] \times 1/O_t$$

In India during the 1960s and early 1970s, a large part of total remittances came through unofficial black market channels. The large gap between the overvalued official exchange rate and the parallel exchange rate in the black market[6] encouraged immigrants to remit large part of their remittances through unofficial channels. After the Indian government started giving favourable terms and facilities for non-resident Indians to open up convertible sterling accounts and external rupees account in the mid 1970s, the unofficial flow of remittances decreased. Since the introduction of economic reforms, the exchange rate policy of freely determined exchange rate reduced the premium on exchanging foreign currency in the black market. Now the premium for exchanging the foreign currency in the foreign exchange rate is just one or two percent more than the market exchange rate. As a result of these policy measures, the unofficial flow of remittances is now very small (Annual flow of remittances into India from abroad is estimated to be in the range of 2 to 2-5 billion U.S. dollars).

Since the exact amount of remittances into Punjab through official and unofficial channels are not available, an attempt has been made in this study to assess the total amount of remittances sent by a sampled group of immigrants since their arrival upto the year 1990. This group of immigrants have also been asked to reveal the mode of utilization of remittances sent.

There are two main theoretical schools which give divergent views regarding the impact of remittances on transforming the agrarian structure. The Neo-classical school[7] treat migration as an escape from poverty. Hence. migrating from low wage region or country to high wage region or country reduce income inequality in the labour exporting regions/countries. Migrants from rural areas also learn skills to work in the industrial sector and hence migration can be considered to promote human capital.

The other school is of the view that migration increases income inequality in rural areas of labour exporting regions/countries.[8] It is argued that migration and hence remittances make migrant family members lazy and hence they make little efforts to increase productivity, resulting in stagnant production. A very small proportion of the income from remittances is used for productivity increasing investment, while a large chunk of the income from remittances is used for meeting daily consumption needs and other non-productive expenditure.

Some empirical studies have been conducted to study the impact of remittances to the Punjab economy. While some studies conclude that foreign remittances have provided additional income which have been largely used for productivity-increasing investment[9], other studies have concluded that emergence of initiative on the part of local entrepreneurs rather than flow of foreign remittances have been largely responsible for increased agricultural and industrial development.[10] At the micro level, the empirical evidence on impact of remittances is inconclusive.

Theorists assume that the poorest migrate and hence remittances are used for consumption and repaying debts. But if a large fraction of immigrants are from middle income class, then it is quite likely that remittances may bc used for enhancing productivity increasing investment. Another factor which will have a bearing on the impact of remittances is the intensity of migration. In a situation where intensity of migration to foreign countries from a particular place is quite large, then a large part of income from remittances are likely to be used for productive investment. Contrarily, if the intensity of migration from a particular place is very low, then there is the possibility of using remittances mainly for consumption purposes.

NOTES AND REFERENCES

1. For details on migration of Indian Labour, see: Panchanan Saha, *Emigration of Indian Labour (1934-1900)*, People's Publishing House, Delhi, 1970.

   Also see: J. Beaujou-Garnier, *Geography of Population,* Longman, London, 1966.

2. See: BA Prakash, "Impact of Foreign Remittances: A case study of Chavakkad village in Kerala" in *Economic and Political Weekly,* XIII: 27, July 8. 1978.

   H K Trivedi and R V Dholakia, *Impact of Foreign Remittances on the Economy of Baladia (District Bhuj Kutch) - A Case Study,* Ahmedabad: Seth Damodardas, School of Commerce, Gujarat University, 1981.

3. See, for example a study by A S Oberai and H K Manmohan Singh (1980), "Migration, Remittance and Rural Development; Findings of a case study in the Indian Punjab", published in *International Labour Review,* Vol. CXIX: 2, March/April.

4. In the sample of 600 male immigrants, only male adults above the age of 18 years at the time of immigration are included in this survey.

5. For estimating recorded and unrecorded remittances, the simple macro economic accounting framework given in the text is taken from a working paper by Richard Brown, "Sudan's Other Economy: Migrants' Remittances, Capital Flight and their Policy Implications," *Sub-Series on Money, Finance and Development,* No. 31, May 1990, Institute of Social Studies, the Hague.

6. During this period, the exchange rate in the black market was nearly double that of official exchange rate.

7. For knowing details about neo-classical thought on this issue, see K. Griffin, "On the Emigration of the Peasantry," *World Development,* Vol. 4, 1976.

8. Views of the second school on this issue are well presented in the article given below:

   H. Rempel and R. Lobdell, "The role of Urban to Rural Remittances in Rural Development," *Journal of Development Studies,* 1978.

   M. Nikolinakos, "Notes Toward a General Theory of Migration in Late Capitalism", *Race and Class, XVII,* 1975.

9. For more favourable views regarding the impact of remittances, see, for example, Bruce La Brack, "The New Patrons: Sikh Overseas" in edited book by N. Gerald Barrier and Verne A. Duesenbery (eds.) *'The Sikh Dias-pora: Migration and the Experience Beyond Punjab,'* *Chanakya Publications,* Delhi, 1989.

10. And for less favourable views, see, for example, T.G. Kessinger, *Vilyatpur 1948-1968: Social and Economic Change in a North Indian Village,* University of California Press, 1974.

    Also see, Roger Ballard, "The Context and Consequences of Migration: Jullundhur and Mirpur compared," *New Community,* Vol. 11, 4, 1983.

3

EMPIRICAL DISCUSSION

In this chapter, an attempt has been made to study the causes of emigration, the educational and skill level of migrants, immigrants' awareness regarding various schemes for attracting foreign remittances, total amount of remittances sent home by the migrants and their uses in the country of their origin, with the help of primary data collected from 540 immigrants settled in the United Kingdom.

Causes of Emigration to the UK

Causes of international migration to a particular country may be economic, political and cultural. Apart from socio-economic causes, the existence of prior links between the sending countries and receiving countries is an important factor for international migration.

Punjabis, particularly the Sikhs, had traditional ties with the British. British rule in India fastened links between Punjabis, particularly the Sikhs who worked in the British Army. So Sikhs mainly from rural areas quickly migrated to the United Kingdom in response to her high demand for semiskilled workers during 1960s. Most of the migrants from Punjab were from cluster of three districts namely Jalandhar, Kapurthala and Hosiarpur. Most of these migrants belonged to middle/lower peasantry class. However during the late 1970s and 1980s, rich peasants started sending their sons for marrying the female spouses of already settled Sikh families in the United Kingdom. After the operation Blue Star in 1984, some people migrated on the basis of seeking political asylum. Later on, migrants went to those areas or cities where their relatives/neighbours/friends had settled. This has given rise to the emergence of Sikhs/Punjabis diaspora.

A number of possible reasons for emigration are listed in Table 3.1. Respondents have been asked to rank causes of emigration. The first three reasons ranked by the respondents are considered in tabulation. Assuming that the first-three ranks have the same weightage, the totals in the last column show that the most dominating cause of emigration from Punjab is the small scale land holdings. In Doaba region of Punjab, most of the upper caste Jat Sikh families have small parcels of land. It is revealed in the survey that a large number of small farmers came to the UK either to enlarge the size of their land holdings or to release mortgage on their land. The second important reason for emigration was the desire to join their families/relatives/friends living in the UK. Thirdly, people also decided to emigrate to take advantage of great opportunities in the UK as revealed by the visible prosperity of returning migrants on occasional short visits to Punjab. Thus it becomes obvious that the dominating force for emigrating to the UK was the weak economic position and the desire for the reunification of the family members, and close relatives and friends.

TABLE 3.1 : Reasons for emigration to the UK

	Rank			
Reasons for Emigration	1	2	3	Total
Small land-holdings	144	138	131	413
Came to UK to join their families/relatives/friends	93	85	98	276
Came to UK to get married to the spouse settled in the UK	25	27	21	73
Unemployment at home	38	34	41	113
Allurement of living abroad	20	24	26	70
Heard about opportunities for prosperity in the UK	87	90	84	261
Desire to provide a more secure future for families	17	16	20	53
Low income in India	56	52	57	165

N = 540

Educational and Skill Level of Migrants at the Time of Migration

Table 3.2 shows that 44 migrants out of 540 possess University degree. A large percentage (76.4) are either High School drop-outs or could not pass the matriculation examination. Ninety-nine respondents did not go to school. The survey also reveals that majority of the migrants were unskilled and were having agricultural background. This finding regarding the education and skill level of migrants from Punjab is in line with OECD's findings which reveal that the level of human capital of migrants to OECD countries is lower than that of natives.

TABLE 3.2 : Education and Skill Level of Migrants at the Time of Migration

	Number of Respondents	%
Those who possessed University degrees	44	8.2
Those who possessed Secondary school certificates	83	15.4
Those who did not possess secondary school certificates	314	58.1
Those who did not receive any formal education	99	18.3
Total	540	100

	Number of Respondents	%
Skilled	32	5.9
Semi-Skilled	78	14.4
Unskilled	430	79.7
Total	540	100

Source: Primary Data

Job Status of Punjabi Immigrants in the UK

It is interesting to know the type of jobs these immigrants are doing in the UK. Table 3.3 reveals their job status. As can be seen in this table, forty-three percent of these immigrants are doing unskilled manual work in factories, foundries, warehouses, airports, construction premises etc. Only fifteen percent are doing skilled jobs like working as welders, fitters, plumbers, painters, technicians, laboratory technicians and drivers etc.. A very small minority (5%) are doing professional jobs such as doctors, engineers, chartered accountants, lawyers, computer programmers and managers etc.. About one-fifth of the immigrants are running their own businesses. Amongst them, a large number are running corner shops. Some are running small workshops, post offices, travel agencies, etc. Very few have been found to be doing wholesale business, like running warehouses, cash and carry, etc.. It was revealed in the survey that a majority of the immigrants bought the corner shops after the mid-seventies. Almost all of those who bought shops were doing factory/manual jobs earlier. Unemployment amongst Punjabi immigrants is fourteen percent which is higher than the national unemployment figure.

Table 3.3 also shows job-status of immigrants immediately after their arrival in UK. As it is obvious from the table, that a majority of them started doing unskilled jobs (factories, foundries warehouses, etc.) A large number of immigrants got employment in dying industries which were facing tough competition from their counterparts in foreign countries. These industries attracted immigrant workers by giving them low wages but plenty of guaranteed overtime. However, with closure or fear of shut down of some of these firms, Punjabi immigrants started looking for their own business or shops, warehouses, post offices, and restaurants, etc. This is borne out by the fact that a number of immigrants doing unskilled jobs declined significantly from 80 per cent in the period immediately after their arrival in the UK to 43 per cent at the present time, and that immigrants in the self-employed category increased sharply from 2 per cent to 19 per cent in the corresponding period. This clearly shows that Punjabi immigrants were good and quick in adapting to new opportunities as compared to indigenous people. This corroborates to the fact that immigrants are the people who are always more entrepreneurial and adventurous.

TABLE 3.3 : Percentage Distribution of Occupational/Job Status of Punjabi Immigrants in the UK

Job status	Per cent of job status at present time	Per cent of job status immediately upon arrival in the UK
Unskilled labour (factory/ foundry, warehouse work, etc.)	43	80
Skilled and technical workers (welders, fitters, plumbers, painters, technicians, carpenters, laboratory technicians, drivers etc..)	15	5
Professional jobs (doctors, engineers, chartered accountants, senior managers, etc..)	5	1
Self-employed (running retail shops, wholesale business, post offices, small workshops, travel agencies, etc..)	19	2
Unemployed	14	4
Not reported	4	8
Total	100	100

N = 540

Immigrants Awareness Regarding Various Schemes for Attracting Foreign Remittances

The need to attract more foreign investment is well recognised both by the state and central government as they are developing programmes to encourage Indians living abroad to send more capital home. The Indian government has developed various schemes—such as priority in allotment of cement, scooters, etc. at controlled prices, offering a higher interest rate to Indians living abroad on their deposits in Non-Resident External Accounts, and loan facilities for making investment in India, etc.. The Indian Government has issued a policy of India Development Bonds (IDBs)[1] for attracting larger inflow of foreign remittances/foreign capital and technology. IBDs are US$ denominated, fully repatriable instruments maturing after 5 years from the date of allotment. They are issued exclusively for non-resident Indians (NRIs). IBDs offer attractive returns, full repatriation benefits, freedom from tax liabilities in India and complete flexibility. In order to know whether Punjabis living abroad are aware of these schemes, this question was put to Punjabi Immigrants. As can be seen from Table 3.4, only forty-one per cent of the respondents stated they were fully aware of various incentives and programmes regarding remittances. More than half (fifty-five percent) are not fully aware of such schemes. Thus there is a desperate need for giving adequate information about such schemes to Punjabi immigrants living in the UK. Such information can be given by placing

TABLE 3.4 : Immigrants' Awareness Regarding India's Government Schemes/Incentives for Attracting Foreign Remittances

Awareness/non-awareness	Percent
Those who are fully aware of Indian government schemes/incentives (such as priority for buying cement, scooters, at controlled prices; higher interest rate on non-resident external accounts; offering loan facilities for investment at low interest rates and provision of raw materials at controlled prices to Indians living abroad who make investment in India, etc.	41
Those who are not fully aware of Indian government schemes/incentives for attracting foreign investment	55
No response	4
Total	100

N = 540

Those immigrants who hold British Passports (British Citizenship) can't buy property in India. Thus, allowing dual citizenship by the Indian government permits increasing remittances to India.

advertisements in the middle of Indian films and programmes shown on British television and through local radio stations which relay songs and other programmes for Asians (like Sunrise Radio in the Middlesex area in the UK). It must be added here that immigrants who hold British passports/British citizenship should be allowed to buy property in India. Furthermore, IDBs scheme which is, at present, reserved for non-residential Indians, should be extended to cover all foreigners. The attractive and alluring feature of IDBs facility would attract even other than non-residential Indians to buy these bonds.

Remittances Sent Home by Immigrants

Immigrants' remittances are of considerable importance in the sense that they provide additional capital and are a source of foreign exchange earnings. Though figures relating to foreign remittances at the national level are available, no such estimates about the magnitude of foreign remittances at the regional level are available. This study makes an attempt in this direction. Percentage distribution of total remittances sent by immigrants since their arrival in the UK is compiled in Table 3.5. As can be seen from the table, the maximum frequencies are in the range of 1.25 to 1.50 lakhs rupees. About fifty percent of the immigrants sent remittances in the range of 0.75 to 1.75 lakh rupees. Only thirteen immigrants sent remittances more than 3 lakhs rupees. Average remittances per reporting immigrant works out to be 1.487 lakhs rupees.[2] By Indian standards, the amount of remittances sent home by Punjabi immigrants is quite high. It must be added that there appears to be an underestimation of the remittance figures because many respondents were hesitant to reveal the true amount of remittances sent home.

It would be interesting to look into the amount of remittances sent home during different decades, and this is given in Table 3.6. As is obvious from this table, only eleven percent of total remittances were sent home during the 1950s. The relatively small amount of remittances sent home during this period can be explained by the fact that only one-tenth of sampled immigrants came to the UK during this period. A large chunk (forty percent) of total remittances were sent during the 1960s. About one-third of total remittances were sent during the 1970s. It is revealed by the immigrants that out of total remittances sent during the 1960s and 1970s, a large amount was sent for building pucca houses, purchasing land and making agricultural improvements. It is disheartening to note the sharp decline in foreign remittances sent home during the 1980s. Only 16 per cent of total remittances were sent during this period.

TABLE 3.5 : Percentage Distribution of Punjabi Immigrants in the UK according to Range of Foreign Remittances Sent Home

Range of foreign remittances sent home (Rs)	Number	Percentage (%)
No remittances/amount of remittance not reported	33	6.11
Below 0.25 lakh	11	2.03
0.25 to 0.50 lakh	23	4.26
0.50 to 0.75 lakh	37	6.85
0.75 to 1.00 lakh	53	9.81
1.00 to 1.25 lakhs	75	13.89
1.25 to 1.50 lakhs	89	16.48
1.50 to 1.75 lakhs	61	11.30
1.75 to 2.00 lakhs	42	7.78
2.00 to 2.25 lakhs	36	6.67
2.25 to 2.50 lakhs	28	5.19
2.50 to 2.75 lakhs	21	3.89
2.75 to 3.00 lakhs	18	3.33
Above 3 lakhs	13	2.41
Average remittance per immigrant (lakhs/Rs.)	1.396	—
Average remittance per reporting (lakhs/Rs.)	1.487	—
Total remittance in Lakhs/Rs	753.8	—

N = 540 One Lakh = 100000

Note: *Remittances figures relate to the total remittances sent home by immigrants since their arrival in the UK to the present time, i.e.; year 1990*

Source: Primary Data

It is revealed in the survey that out of the total remittances sent during the 1980s, a very small amount was sent for building pucca houses/ purchasing land in the native villages, and a fairly large amount was sent for purposes like marriage and religious ceremonies, for making deposits in Indian banks and setting up cooperative/private buses and loan companies. A vast majority of sampled immigrants revealed that they sent fairly large amounts of money during the 1960s and 1970s for building pucca houses/purchasing land/making agricultural improvements, because they initially had the intention of going back home for good after staying a few years in the UK. It is claimed by them that since they no longer want to return home for settlement, there is no point in sending money home for such purposes. Instead they should and they are actually using the money for making their lives more easy and comfortable in the UK.

TABLE 3.6 : Decadewise Percentage Distribution of Foreign Remittances Sent Home

Period	Percentage
1951-1960	11
1961-1970	40
1971-1980	33
1981-1990	16
Total	100

Purposes/Utilization of Remittances Sent Home

Having known the amount of remittances sent home, it is important to know purposes/utilization[3] for which foreign remittances were sent home. It seems worthwhile to know whether remittances have been used for productive/consumptive purposes. Percentage distribution of remittances sent home is compiled in Table 3.7.

Priority list obtained from migrants for utilising remittances is given as follows: (i) productivity increasing agricultural improvement by buying tractors and other farm machinery, livestock, fertiliser and installing tubewells[4], (ii) purchase of land, (iii) construction/repair of houses, (iv) bank deposits, (v) business investment in small scale industries, cooperative buses and finance companies, (vi) public works—construction of pucca roads in and around the village, primary schools and public buildings for village weddings.

Twenty-nine percent of total remittances have been sent/used for making agricultural improvements. It is revealed in the survey that out of total remittances sent for agricultural improvements, a large amount was used for buying tractors, farm machinery and installing tubewells/ electric pumpsets. Some remittances were sent to buy chemical fertilizers, improved seeds, insecticides and pesticides. Thus remittances sent home have helped generating agricultural capital locally. According to this study, in Punjab twenty-nine percent of total remittances have been used for making agricultural improvements[5], while it is uncommon for emigrants from Gujarat and Kerala to invest in agriculture.[6] The reason for the difference can be explained by the fact that because of good soil conditions and easy accessibility of water in

TABLE 3.7 : Percentage Distribution of Purposes/Utilization of Foreign Remittances Sent Home

Purposes/utilization for which foreign remittances were sent home	Percentage (%)
Family maintenance	8
Marriages, religious and social ceremonies like Akhand Path or Kirtan and death feasts, etc..	5
Construction/repair of houses	12
Purchase of land	14
Agricultural improvements for buying tractors, other farm machinery, livestock, chemicals, fertilizers, new seeds and installing tubewells (electric pump sets), etc..	29
Business investment in small scale industries, setting up cooperative buses and loan/finance companies	9
Bank deposits	12
Public works—elementary school, public buildings for village weddings and public celebrations, paving village roads and construction of temple (gurdwara), etc..	5
Others	6
Total	100

almost the whole (ninety percent) of Punjab, investment in agricultural activities bring high return, whereas in the case of Gujarat, because of less fertile land and lack of easy accessibility of water in large parts of these states, investment in agricultural activities may not bring high returns. Remittances (fourteen percent) were also sent for purchasing land. Respondents mentioned that they had sent money home in order to enlarge the size of land holdings. In the village culture of Punjab, the bigger the size of land holdings,.the higher the honour of the family. Thus in order to increase the prestige of the family, immigrants sent remittances to purchase land mainly during the late 1960s and 1970s.

Another major use of foreign remittances was the construction of large houses. It is revealed in the survey that initially some immigrants sent money home to build well-designed large houses on the outskirts of the villages where they are easily noticeable. Then other immigrants followed them because it was degrading to family prestige not to build a large house in the village. It is revealed that a large number of these houses were built during the late 1960s and early 1970s. Since initially the immigrants, after staying a few years in the UK, wanted to return eventually to Punjab, they sent money to build large houses where they could live. an easy and comfortable life. In some cases, money was sent for repairs and for making extensions of one or two rooms to their existing houses.

It is worth knowing as to whether Punjabi immigrants did not have the intention of bringing their families into the U.K. at all or they wanted to bring their families into the U.K. after properly settling down in the U.K. It was revealed by immigrants that they were fully intended to bring their families into the U.K., but the fear of restrictive immigration barriers created mad rush for bringing their families into the U.K. at the earliest. Some immigrants revealed that even after bringing their families into the U.K. they had the intention of going back home for settlement after staying a few years in the U.K. Thus Punjabi immigrants attitude in this regard is different from those of Morocco immigrants into France where they never thought of bringing their wives and children into France. Morocco immigrants stayed alone in France and sent savings/ remittances back home which were mainly used for daily needs, replacing kacha houses by pucca houses and farming improvements, etc.

It is seen that five percent of remittances were sent for marriages, religious and social ceremonies. Respondents stated that they had sent money home for meeting the dowry and other expenses on weddings of their sister/brother/daughter/son and next of kin group. When immigrants return home for short visits, it is a ritual for the returning immigrants to perform religious ceremonies like 'Akhand Path'/'Kirtan'[7]. These religious ceremonies are done to demonstrate gratitude to God for good fortune. Remittances were also sent for giving death feasts to relatives and friends at the time of elderly people's death.

Eight per cent of total remittances were sent for family maintenance. Since immigrants did not initially bring their families to the UK, money was sent to support wife, children and needy parents. With the emigration of their dependents to the UK, this type of remittance ceased. In very rare cases, money was sent to support the family maintenance of the nearest kin.

Some money (five percent) was sent for public works like constructing temples (gurdwara), public buildings for village weddings and public celebrations, paving village roads, building rooms and the purchase of furniture for primary and middle schools.

A part of foreign remittances (9%) was sent for making investment in small scale industries, co-operative buses and finance/loan companies.

About one-eighth (12%) of the remittances was sent for making deposits in Indian banks. A large number of immigrants have deposited money in Indian banks. Some immigrants have opened Non Resident External Accounts which give them a higher interest rate as compared to the interest rate given on internal accounts. Many immigrants have kept their money in both fixed and current account deposits. Though the interest rate on the savings account deposits is low, but they keep the money (it is revealed by immigrants) in the savings account deposit for the simple reason that they can withdraw the money immediately when they go to Punjab for short visits (four or five weeks) after every two or three years.

It needs to be mentioned here that seventeen percent of remittances have been used on marriage, religious and social ceremonies, and for constructing large houses on the outskirts of their villages. It is revealed that in the majority of these houses, none of their close family members are living. Thus many well-designed large houses are lying idle, while in very few houses some next of kin are living. Some of these houses are occupied by school teachers, ..., and other government employees who either live free of charge or pay very low or nominal rent. Thus money spent by the immigrants on these houses is unproductive as it does not give any return on investment. Also money spent by immigrants lavishly on marriages, death feasts, etc. comes under conspicuous consumption.[8]

Obviously, foreign remittances sent for purposes such as agricultural improvements, small scale business investment and bank deposits (which is 50 percent) are productive in the sense that they bring return on investment. With the help of foreign remittances, cultivators in Punjab have been able to install tubewells, buy chemical fertilizers and new seeds. Thus remittances sent by immigrants for agricultural improvements have helped generate agricultural capital in Punjab.

It is clear from the mode of utilization figures given in table that the bulk of overseas remittances was used for productive purposes. A further clue of using remittances for productivity increasing investment is obtained from the positive correlation between migrant families and tractor owning families in our sampled villages.[9] Majority of migrants revealed that they bought Massey Ferguson tractors by making payment in cash.

Immigration Promotes Capitalist Relations in Punjab Agriculture

International migration and hence remittances also appear to have strengthened the development of capitalist relations in Punjab agriculture. Since migrant families have acquired more agricultural machinery like tractors, trolleys and combine harvestors etc. as compared to non-migrant families, one can argue that migration has increased the concentration of assets in rural Punjab. As the land ceiling in Punjab is only on ownership of land and not on operational size of land holding, rich farmers have leased-in land from the migrant families. Hence migration has helped increasing the operational size of land holding of rich farmers. It may be mentioned here that migrant families prefer to lease-out land to rich farmers as compared to poor farmers because the former do not default and pay higher rent. Because of the apprehension of losing ownership of land, some migrant families have lately started mortgaging their land and in some cases they have started selling their lands.

Remittances increased Effective Demand for Consumer Goods

While analysing the role of remittances, one should not forget the multiple effect of remittances in generating income and employment. In the villages under study, it is seen that migrant families tend to have more consumer goods like scooters, mopeds, refrigerators and expensive furniture items. Thus overseas remittances have increased the effective demand for many consumer goods which in turn, through its multiple effect, must have resulted in generating more income and employment opportunities.

Inflow of Remittances and the Exchange Rate

The economic theory suggests that remittances may help strengthening the exchange rate. More availability of foreign currency through official channels should strengthen the exchange rate. Thus it is obvious that inflow of remittances through official channels must have created positive effects on India's balance of payments and thus has reduced the necessity of devaluing Indian rupee.

Remittances Escalate Land Prices

Foreign remittances appear to have pushed up prices of land in rural Punjab. Since acquiring more land by family is a status symbol, greater competition among the migrant families to purchase land adjacent to their farms must have pushed up land prices considerably especially during 1960s and 1970s when substantial amount of remittances came into Punjab through unofficial black channels.

One can argue that since remittances is just one component of household income, it may be difficult to discover the different ways in which remittances are utilized. Since in this study we have tried to know the uses of remittances from immigrants settled in the U.K., the mode of utilization of remittances as revealed by the immigrants can be said to reflect true position regarding modes of utilization. It may also be argued that some income generated through the use of new agricultural technology must have been used for productivity increasing investment. From the foregoing discussion, it may be concluded that a higher income of the rural household made possible through substantial amount of overseas remittances have helped in uplifting the rural economy of Punjab.

However one cannot generalise that what is true about this mode of utilisation of remittances in the villages of central Punjab is going to be true for other parts of the country. For example, a study relating to a village in Maharashtra[10] clearly brings out that a large percentage of remittances had been spent on luxury consumer goods. For making more accurate analysis of the effects of remittances, it would be more appropriate to compare the economic and social progress made in villages from where many people have migrated to that of villages from where no migration has taken place.

The empirical evidence regarding the mode of utilization of overseas remittances resulting from micro-level study based on some villages in central Punjab reveals that the large percentage of remittances have been spent for productive uses. Thus the results of this study support the 'accumulation' rather than 'survivalist' theory. The mode of utilization of remittances seems to be affected by the absolute value of remittances and the economic status of immigrants. If the absolute value of remittances is small, then a large part of remittances is likely to be spent for meeting consumption needs. On the contrary, if the absolute values of remittances is large, then, even after meeting minimum consumption needs, large left over remittances are likely to be used for productive purposes.

Further if the poorest migrate, then bulk of remittances are most likely to be used for consumption. On the other hand if the majority of immigrants belong to middle class and have reasonably good economic position, then a large percentage of remittances are likely to be spent for productive uses. Since majority of the migrants from central Punjab are from the middle peasant proprietor class and the absolute value of overseas remittances being substantial, a large part of remittances were spent on productive uses. Although study has not examined the effect of unskilled migrants on British workers' wages and employment, but it is revealed by immigrants that many of them worked on lower wages than British workers, and this must have increased the profits of entrepreneurs which in turn would have resulted in higher investment and higher growth in the host country.

NOTES AND REFERENCES

1. See pamphlet entitled "India Development Bonds", issued by State Bank of India obtained from India's High Commission in the U.K. India Development Bonds (IDBs) provide an exciting new deport avenue. They incorporate all the attractive features of NRI Bonds (second series) and quite a few new features as is evident from the following:
   (a) The definition of NRIs now includes spouse of NRIs (not only wife as was the case earlier).
   (b) Overseas Corporate Bodies where NRIs have control are permitted to purchase IDBs.
   (c) Banks acting in fiduciary capacity on behalf of NRIs and OCBs can purchase IDBs without disclosing the names of NRIs and OCBs.
   (d) Both principal and interest are fully repatriable.
   (e) IDBs can be sold to persons residents in India against non-repatriable Indian Rupees.
   (f) IDBs are also transferable among persons resident in India.
   (g) IDBs are also available in US Dollars 50,000.

   The different attributes of IDBs combine to make them an ideal instrument of deposit. The unique package of full repatriation, allowance for full amnesty and immunity (NRIs/OCBs and First resident Donee will not be required to disclose the nature and source of deposit nor be subject to any enquiry of investigation), low facility, choice of cumulative, non-cumulative (half yearly) interest payment, joint holding facility, procedural simplicity, attractive returns, protection against any likely loss in the exchange value of the Indian Rupee vis-a-vis US Dollar, exemption from Indian tax liabilities, provision of premature encashment, free transferability between NRIs as well as Indians and facility of gifting caters to all major expectations any NRI would have from a good deposit.

2. It needs to be mentioned here that contribution to remittances sent home is not only of male immigrants but also of their wives and children.

3. It is revealed by immigrants that almost the entire amount of money sent home was actually used for the same purpose for which it was sent. In other words, almost the entire amount of remittances were utilized for the same purpose for which they were sent.

4. Tubewells are a fast source of pumping water for irrigation. It consists of a four/six inch pipe, a pump and an electric motor. Prior to tubewells, traditional/persian wheel type wells driven by bullocks were the slow form of pumping water for irrigation. Thus, a fast source of irrigation made possible

by tubewells, together with new high yielding varieties of seeds and chemical fertilizers helped to revolutionise agriculture in Punjab.

5. Oberai and Singh's study (*Ibid.*) also shows that remittances in Indian Punjab are used extensively for making farm improvements and purchasing land.

6. See: Prakash's Study (*Ibid.*) for Kerala and Trivedi and Dholakia's study *(Ibid.)* for Gujarat.

7. 'Akhand Path' is a religious ceremony. After reciting the whole holy book (Granth Sahib) continuously, for which it takes twenty-four hours, the feast is given to close and prominent villagers, relative and friends. For performing 'Kirtan' ceremony, religious songs (hymns) are sung for three/four hours, then a tea party is given to some close villagers and friends. Thus both 'Akhand Path' and 'Kirtan' are forms of worship.

8. It was revealed by immigrants that pattern and purposes of remittances changed over the course of time. In the first phase, remittances were sent mainly for family maintenance and for making agricultural improvements. During the second phase, remittances were sent for purposes like constructing large houses in the villages, weddings, public works and religious ceremonies. Remittances during the third phase assumed a new purpose, e.g.: investment in small scale industries, running finance/loan company and bank deposits. Thus, pattern and purposes of remittances have followed different stages of developmental process. For details about different stages of developmental process, see J.R. Goody (1958), *Domestic Developmental Cycle in Groups,* Cambridge: Cambridge University Press.

9. The correlation coefficient between migrant families and tractor owning families has been found to be 0.53.

10. A study relating to Baladiya village in Maharashtra reveals that the bulk of foreign remittances has been spent on luxury consumer goods. For details, see Venkat Narayan, "Poor Millionaires" *Sunday Times,* London, January 18, 1975.

4

ASSIMILATION PROBLEMS AND OTHER ASPECTS OF PUNJABI IMMIGRANTS IN THE U.K.

When people migrate from India to U.K., they find themselves in a completely different culture. That is why they take some time to settle down and assimilate the culture of the foreign country. So the present chapter discusses assimilation problems of immigrants and the retainment of Indian cultural values by immigrants' children abroad.

Housing Status of Punjabi Immigrants

To own a house with no mortgage or easily payable mortgage is a good indication of the financial position of a person. It is, therefore, interesting to know the housing status of Punjabi immigrants in the UK and this is compiled in Table 4.1. It can be seen that 58 per cent of immigrants have either no mortgage or less than £ 15000 of a mortgage pay. Only eight percent of the people have more than £ 45000 of a mortgage to pay. It is revealed in the sruvey that almost all house-owners who have more than a £ 45000 standing mortgage came to the UK after the mid-seventies and they bought their houses during the eighties. Eighty-four per cent immigrants own their houses and only sixteen per cent are living either in rented (council and private) accommodation or are living with their friends or relatives.

Immigrants' Rating of Various Aspects of Life in UK

Having spent a few years in UK it is interesting to see how Punjabi immigrants view various aspects of life in the UK. Various aspects of life in the UK have been listed in the questionnaire and the respondents have been asked to rate these aspects. Their views are tabulated in

TABLE 4.1 : Percentage Distribution of Housing Status of Punjabi Immigrants in the UK

Living Status	Per cent	Percentage distribution of standing mortgage on owner occupied houses					
		No mortgage to pay	Less than £15000 mortgage to pay	£15000 to £30000 mortgage to pay	£30000 to £45000 mortgage to pay	Above £45000 mortgage to pay	Total
Owner Occupation	84						
Council renting	7						
Private renting	5						
Living with friends or relatives	4						
Total	100	12	46	20	14	8	100

N = 540

Table 4.2. It is to be seen from the table that three hundred and twenty-five respondents (60.2 per cent) respondents consider monetary advantage as good. Only thirty-five (6.5 per cent) respondents consider monetary advantage as poor. As regards communication and transportation facilities, clean and healthy environment, access to education, a large majority of the respondents rated these aspects as either excellent or good. In striking contrast, a large number of the respondents viewed fair treatment at work, social adjustment of self and family as either satisfactory or poor. Three hundred and forty-two (63.3 per cent) and one hundred and twenty-three (22.8 per cent) respondents rate the standard of living in the UK as good and satisfactory respectively.

Assimilation Problems of Immigrations

Having spent quite a few years in UK, it is interesting to identify assimilation problem[1] being faced by Punjabi immigrants in the UK. A number of possible problems of assimilation have been listed in the questionnaire and respondents have been asked to rank the problems. The first-three problems given by the respondents are compiled in the Table 4.3. Totals have been given in the last column, assuming that the first-three ranks have the same weightage. It is obvious from the totals

TABLE 4.2 : Rating of Various Aspects of Life in the UK by Punjabi Immigrants

Aspects of life	Excellent	Good	Satis-factory	Poor	No response	Total
Monetary advantage	70	325	90	35	20	540
Fair treatment at work	12	86	198	229	15	540
Communi-cations and transportation facilities	216	159	121	19	25	540
Clean and healthy environment	207	183	88	33	29	540
Access to education	176	223	81	28	32	540
Standard of living	58	342	123	5	12	540
Social adjustment of self and family	14	36	259	212	19	540

N = 540

given in the last column that the most important assimilation problem relates to cultural reasons/cultural incongruence. Other assimilation problems, in order of importance, are (a) treated as second class citizens (feeling of discrimination when looking for jobs, promotion in jobs, etc.); (b) difficult to develop meaningful relations with English people and (c) language problems. Perhaps it is worth mentioning that Punjabi immigrants have not been able to assimilate into British culture partly because of racial discrimination, language problem, etc. and partly because they are having the reference group back at home with whom they are keeping ties and are sharing cultural values with them. In contrast to immigrants, British born young Punjabis are having little or no assimilation problems because of the fact that they have the British reference group from whom they borrow cultural values and that they have very little or no ties with people in India. However, it is revealed in the Survey that even British born young Punjabis are facing discrimination in terms of getting employment, promotion etc. This must be stopped for making the younger generation to assimilate fully into British culture.

TABLE 4.3 : Assimilation Problems of Punjabi Immigrants in the UK

Problems	Rank			
	1	2	3	Total
Cultural reasons/cultural incongruence	130	125	128	383
Language Problem	55	71	65	191
No feeling of uniqueness	24	20	26	70
Difficult to develop meaningful relations with English people	74	69	70	213
Lack of involvement in public affairs	20	19	18	57
Treated as second class citizens (feeling of discrimination in job-finding, promotion in job, etc.)	101	98	103	302
Mechanical/very busy life in UK	17	13	10	40

N = 540

Immigrants' Decision Not To Return Home

Initially, the majority of the immigrants had the intention of eventually going home for settlement. After having spent a number of years in the UK, a large number of immigrants (seventy-six per cent) do not want to return home for settlement. These immigrants have been asked to rank reasons for not wanting to return home. The first-three reasons have been tabulated in Table 4.4. From the totals given in the last column (assuming that the first-three ranks have the same weightage) it is clear that the most dominating reason for not returning home for settlement is comfortable living standards in the UK. Other reasons, in order of importance, are (i) their children do not want to go to India for settlement (and the parents want to stay with their children; (ii) unsafe, uncongenial, risky environment in India, (iii) corrupt, unresponsive and bureaucratic administration in India, etc.

Immigrants' Decision to Return Home for Settlement

When immigrants were asked about returning home for settlement[2], some of them (24%) stated that they wanted to go home for settlement. It is interesting to see why some immigrants, after having lived so many years in the UK, want to return home for settlement. Possible reasons for this are listed in Table 4.5. The first-three reasons given by the respondents are compiled and totals (assuming that the first-three ranks

TABLE 4.4 : Reasons for Decision of Immigrants Not to Return Home for Settlement

Reasons	Rank 1	2	3	Total
Adjusted well in the UK	30	33	28	91
No future for children in India for getting employment, etc.	27	22	25	74
Comfortable living standards in UK	91	85	89	265
Unripe, uncongenial, risky, environment in India	58	63	51	172
Hierarchical nature of organisation in India	5	2	4	11
Poor transport and communication systems in India	10	11	7	28
Corrupt, unresponsive, bureaucratic administration in India	41	43	46	130
No access to good educational facilities in India	11	8	7	26
Children don't want to go to India for settlement and the parents want to stay with/near their children	73	70	76	219
Wives don't want to go to India for settlement	34	25	27	86

N = 410 (75.9%)

have same weightage) are given in the last column. It is clear from the totals that the most important reason for the desire to return is strong kin and family ties in India. Other important reasons are (i) fear of children going astray; (ii) negative experiences encountered in the UK (such as racial discrimination and being treated as second class citizens; and (iii) cultural reasons.

Immigrant Children's Decision Not to Return to India for Settlement

As some of the immigrants claimed that the main reason for their not returning home for settlement is that their children did not want to go to India for settlement. It seems therefore, worthwhile to know why immigrants' children do not want to go to India for settlement. Children were asked to rank reasons for their decisions not to go to India for settlement. The first-three reasons given by the respondents are compiled and totals (assuming that the first-three ranks have the same weightage) are given in the last column (see Table 4.6). It is clear from the totals that the most dominant reasons for not going to India for settlement is more

TABLE 4.5 : Reasons for Immigrants' Decision to Return Home

Reasons	Rank			
	1	2	3	Total
Strong kin and family ties in India	22	20	25	67
Familiarity with environments and roots in India	9	7	5	21
Cultural reasons/cultural incongruence	15	18	13	46
Negative experiences encountered in the UK such as racial discrimination and treated as second class citizens	17	14	20	51
Fear of children going astray	18	23	21	62
Mechanical/very busy life in UK	12	11	15	38
Lonely life especially after retirement	5	4	2	11
Privileged family background—wealth, power and status	10	11	13	34
British weather (being cold and humid) is unsuitable for aged person	4	3	1	8

N = 130

familiarity with the British way of life (as compared to the Indian way of life). Other important reasons, in order of importance, are (i) comfortable living standard in the UK; (ii) unsafe, uncongenial, risky environment in India; and (iv) would not be able to get the right job.

Level of Education attained by Immigrants' Children

Parents are always well-wishers of their children. It is their natural instinct that their children should get respectable and well-paid positions in their career. It is, therefore, worthwhile to know the level of education attained by immigrants' children in the UK and this is shown in Table 4.7. It can be seen that fifty-six per cent of children have given up education after passing their GCSE examinations. Nine per cent have done apprenticeship courses like electrical, mechanical and civil engineering, etc. Four per cent have successfully completed professional courses like M.B.B.S., Chartered Accountancy, M.B.A., Law degree, etc.. Thus, altogether twenty-four per cent of immigrants have been successful in their mission to give higher education to their children.

TABLE 4.6 : Reasons for Immigrants' Children's Decision not to go to India for Settlement

Reasons	Rank			
	1	2	3	Total
More familiarity with British way of life as compared to Indian way of life	83	80	89	252
Comfortable living standard in UK	66	61	64	191
Low and inadequate pay in India	29	28	24	81
Would not be able to get the right job	38	35	41	114
Unsafe, uncongenial, risky environment in India	40	45	38	123
Would not be able to adjust to Indian living conditions	44	49	43	136
Inadequate transportation and communication facilities in India	13	10	9	32
No access to good educational facilities	22	18	17	57
Corrupt, unresponsive bureaucracy in India	35	39	33	107
Ugly, dirty, crowded urban environment	10	7	6	23

N = 450

Retainment of Indian Cultural Values of Immigrants' Children

It is interesting to know whether immigrants' children (the so-called second generation),[3] are maintaining Indian cultural values in the UK. Since the majority of women in Indian Punjab do not drink alcohol, do not smoke, do not eat meat (especially beef), do not have boyfriends, do not wear skirts, and majority of them go to the temple, do household chores (knitting, sewing etc..), wear *salwar-kameeze,* one should study the behaviour of young girls in the UK in relation to these things.

As majority of young girls in the UK stated that they do not smoke, do not drink alcohol, do not eat beef, do not have boyfriends, do not go to disco parties, do go to the temple, wear salwar-kameeze, do household chores, it indicates that the 'second generation' young girls are maintaining the values of ethnic culture in the UK (see Table 4.8).

It needs to be mentioned here that since about one-third of young girls wear skirts, have boyfriends openly and secretly, go to disco parties

TABLE 4.7 : Percentage Distribution of Level of Education Attained by Immigrants' Children

Level of education	Percent
GCSE	56
Apprenticeship courses	9
Ordinary levels ('O' Levels)	10
Advanced levels ('A' Levels)	8
Bachelor Degree	7
Master Degree	5
Professional courses such as MBBS, Chartered Accountancy, Law Degree, etc.	4
No response	1
Total	100

N = 450

openly and secretly, these girls are breaking Indian traditions in these matters. So it seems likely that in the future young girls may not maintain the values of ethnic culture.

Arranged Marriage

Already some research on 'arranged marriage' amongst Sikhs in the UK has been carried out by people like Ballard, R and Ballard, C (1977), Helweg, AW (1979).[4] As arranged marriage is not uncommon in Indian Punjab, it is interesting to know the views of immigrants' children about arranged marriage. Of a sample of four hundred young girls and boys, a vast majority of the respondents are expecting to have an arranged marriage. Only ten per cent of the respondents said that they were determined to have a love marriage even if it destroyed their relations with their parents.

A typical quote of those who are in favour of arranged marriage and who are looking forward to arranged marriage is:

> "Arranged marriages are successful and divorces are very rare. But love marriages are a failure. In a majority of cases, divorces happen after a few years. Arranged marriage is better because parents, being experienced in worldly matters, help in choosing the right match. All the arranged marriages in our family circle have been successful. So we are looking forward to arranged marriage".

It needs to be mentioned here that although ninety percent of the respondents are expecting to have an arranged marriage, but thirty-

TABLE 4.8 : The Maintenance/Non-Maintenance of Ethnic Culture by Young Punjabi Girls in UK

Cultural Values	Yes Percent	No Percent
Cigarettes	1	99
Alcohol	14	86
Beef	17	83
Going to temple	89	11
Wearing traditional dress (salwar-kameeze)	81	19
Household chores (knitting, sewing, etc.)	97	3
Wearing skirts	36	64
Having boyfriends	33	67
Hindi songs	92	8
English songs and music	68	32
Going to disco parties	34	66
Seeing videos of Indian films	93	7
Punjabi language	100	Nil

N = 200

five percent of them, nevertheless no longer support the arranged marriage. The following quote illustrates this point:

> "I think love marriages are best because you love the person with whom you are going to marry, but my parents would not allow this. So I would not go for a love marriage because its consequences are too great. Everybody in the family and close friends circle can be hurt and I will destroy my relations with my parents and consequently will lose my parents' love which I do not want. Also nobody will want to marry my sister."

Thus it is obvious that British born young Punjabis' perceptions regarding arranged marriage have changed because the majority of them wanted to have love marriage. But they are not going for love marriage because of the family constraints. So it appears that love marriage on a large scale will start taking after some years because changes in value precede changes in behaviour by quite a few years.

NOTES AND REFERENCES

1. Definition of assimilation relates to adjustment of Punjabi immigrants into British Society. Of course, Punjabis are mixing up with other Punjabi groups

consisting of their neighbours, their friends and relatives living in the same or other towns. But here we are concerned with intermingling of Punjabi immigrants with plural society/British people.

2. One can question here that when a vast majority of immigrants are owning their own houses in the UK, how can they have, then, the desire to return home for settlement? This question can be answered by the fact that owing a house in the UK is not a deterrent for immigrants to return home for settlement because a house is an encashable property which can be easily sold at any time.

3. The term 'second generation' relates to children of immigrants who are born in the UK or who came to UK when they were under five years of age.

4. See, for example: Ballard, R and Ballard, C (1977), "The Sikhs: The Development of South Asian Settlements in Britain", in J. Watson (edited 1977), Between Two Centuries: *Migrants and Minorities in Britain,* Oxford, Basil, Blackwell.

   Helweg, AW (1979), *Sikhs in England,* Delhi: Oxford University Press.

5

SUMMARY

In this chapter, an attempt has been made to present a brief summary of the empirical findings.

The study brings out various findings which are listed below:

(a) Amongst causes of emigration, the most dominant reason for Punjabis to emigrate to the UK was the weak economic position (due to small land holdings) and the desire for the unification of the family members and close relatives and friends.

(b) At the time of migration, a majority of migrants from Punjab were either high-school drop-outs or did not go to school. They were doing unskilled farming jobs.

(c) A majority of Punjabi immigrants are either doing unskilled manual jobs or running corner shops and other small businesses like post offices, travel agencies, small workshops and warehouses, etc. Only fifteen and five percent are doing skilled and professional jobs respectively.

(d) Remittances sent home by immigrants since their arrival in the UK have been found to be around 1.5 lakhs rupees per immigrant. About fifty percent of the immigrants sent remittances in the range of 0.75 to 1.75 lakhs rupees. The actual remittances per immigrant might be more because some immigrants showed hesitation to reveal the remittances' figure. By Indian standards, the amount of remittances sent home is quite high. The decadewise percentage distribution of foreign remittances sent home was 11 percent during the 1950s, 40 percent during the 1960s, 33 percent during the 1970s, and 16 percent during the 1980s. It is revealed by immigrants that during the 1960s and the 1970s they sent fairly large amounts of money for building pucca houses, purchase of land and agricultural improvements because initially they had the desire to return home for settlement. The relatively small amount of money that was sent home during the 1980s can be explained by the fact that they did not send money for such purposes during this period. Out of the total remittances sent homes during the 1980s, a large amount was sent for marriage and religious ceremonies, and for making investments and deposits in India, etc.

(e) Seventeen percent of the total remittances have been sent/ used for unproductive purposes like marriages, religious and social ceremonies, and for constructing large houses on the outskirts of the villages in which no close family member of the immigrants' family is living. These well designed large houses are lying idle or some government employees are either living free of the charge or paying very low or nominal rent. Fourteen percent of remittances have been sent for purchasing land.

Twenty-nine percent of total remittances have been used for making agricultural improvements, i.e.: installing tubewells (electric pumpsets), buying chemical fertilizers, new seeds, tractors and other farm machinery. Some remittances have been sent for purposes like bank deposits (twelve percent), co-operative buses and finance companies (nine percent), public works (five percent) and family maintenance (eight percent) respectively.

(f) A majority of immigrants (fifty-five percent) are not fully aware of the schemes and incentives introduced by the Indian government to attract foreign remittances. The need for making immigrants fully aware of such schemes should be at the top of the priority list of Indian government programmes.

(g) Eighty-four percent of immigrants live in their own houses and fifty-eight percent out of them have either no mortgage to pay or less than £ 15000 left of their mortgage to pay.

(h) A majority of the immigrants rated monetary advantage, communication and transportation facilities, clean and healthy environment, access to education, as good, while a large number of respondents stated that fair treatment at work, social adjustment of self and family, as either satisfactory or poor.

(i) The most important assimilation problem of Punjabi immigrants relates to cultural reasons/cultural incongruence.

Other assimilation problems in order of importance are (a) treated as second class citizens; (b) difficult to develop meaningful relations with English people and (c) language problem.

(j) The most dominating reason for immigrants decisions not to return home for settlement, is the comfortable living standards in the UK. Other reasons, in order of importance are (a) their children do not want to go to India for settlement (and the parents want to stay with/near their children); (b) unsafe, uncongenial and risky environment in India; and (c) corrupt, unresponsive and bureaucratic administration in India.

(k) For those (twenty-four percent) who want to return to India for settlement, important reasons for their decision to return have been found to be (a) strong kin and family ties in India; (b) fear of children going astray; (c) negative experiences encountered in the UK and (d) cultural reasons.

(l) Regarding immigrants' children, the most dominant reason for not going to India for settlement is more familiarity with the British way of life as compared to the Indian way of life. Other important reasons, in order of importance, are (a) comfortable living standards in the UK; (b) would not be able to adjust to Indian living conditions; (c) unsafe, uncongenial, risky environment to India and (d) would not be able to get the right job.

(m) Fifty-six percent of immigrants' children have given up education after passing their GCSE examinations. Only twenty-four percent have attained education up to and above advanced level. Four percent have successfully completed professional courses like M.B.A., MBBS, Chartered Accountancy, Law Degree, etc.. Nine percent have done apprenticeship courses.

(n) Although a majority of 'second generation' young girls in the UK are maintaining Indian cultural values, one-third of young girls are not maintaining these values of ethnic culture in matters like (a) not having boyfriends; (b) by not going to disco parties and (c) by not wearing skirts.

Though a big majority of young girls and boys (ninety percent) expect to have arranged (traditional) marriages, thirty-five percent of them no longer support arranged marriage. Only a very small minority (ten percent) want to go ahead for a love marriage even if it destroyed their relations with their parents.

The following influence can be drawn from the above discussion. A vast majority of sampled immigrants revealed that they sent a fairly large amount of money during 1960s and 1970s for building pucca houses/ purchasing land/making agricultural improvements, because they initially had the intention of going back home for settlement after staying a few years in the UK. It is pointed out by them since they no longer have the desire to return home for settlement, there is no point in sending money home for such purposes. Instead, they (immigrants) should and are actually using the money for making their houses more easy and comfortable in the U.K. So it is quite obvious that Punjabi immigrants, at the present time, can be expected, and/or persuaded to send money at homes only for other than the above-mentioned (building pucca houses/ purchasing land/making agricultural improvements) purposes like making investment and depositing money in India, etc. For this to happen, the Indian government should provide them with generous loan and other facilities and should create a congenial atmosphere for making investment in India. Since the majority of immigrants are not fully aware of various Indian government incentives and schemes (including IDBs scheme) regarding making investment and depositing money, in India, there is a desperate need for giving intensive publicity for such schemes. Perhaps it may be worthwhile to hire some insurance company which can drive home the good points of various Indian government schemes and programmes through personal visits.

As IDBs scheme is quite attractive and alluring, this facility which is reserved at present only for non-residential Indians, should be extended to cover all foreigners irrespective of the fact of whether they are of Indian origin or not. Also, the Indian government should allow British/American/Canadian citizens to buy property in India. Since the law and order situation in India is a serious deterrent for making investment in India, the law and order situation should be greatly improved. The Indian government should make sincere efforts to find an amicable solution for such problems. All these measures would help to increase the flow of remittances into India.

As it is revealed in the survey that British born immigrants' children have been experiencing much racial discrimination when finding jobs and promotion, etc. the British government should immediately take concrete steps to stop this happening. This would enable young Punjabis to integrate fully into British society and thus they would make a full contribution to the growth of the British economy.

APPENDIX

QUESTIONNAIRE

1 General Information

1.1 Name and address of immigrant ______________________

1.2 Arrival in UK: When? ______________________

1.3 Why did you come to this town?
relatives □ friends □ more chances of getting job because of:
(a) industrial centre □ (b) near airport □ (c) near dockyard □

1.4 Citizenship: British □ Indian □ Other ____________

1.5 Religion: Sikh □ Hindu □ Muslim □ Christian □ Jain □ Other □

1.6 Mother tongue: Punjabi □ Hindi □ Urdu □
Other □

1.7 Caste: Jat □ Harijan □ Ramgarhia □ Khatri □ Brahmin □ Ramadasia □ Balmiki □

1.8 Married □ Unmarried □ Widowed □

1.9 Number of Children: Boys__________ Girls__________

1.10 Age groups

	Boys		Girls	
	0-10	□	0-10	□
	10-16	□	10-16	□
	17-21	□	17-21	□
	Over 21	□	Over 21	□

1.11 Did the family come with you to the UK? Yes □ No □

1.12 Did you have the intention of bringing your family into UK:
Immediately □ After settling down properly in UK □

Not at all ☐

1.13 Did the enforcement of fear of strict immigration barriers make you rush to bring your family into UK?

Yes ☐ No ☐

2. Reasons for Emigrating to UK

2.1 State reasons for coming to UK (Please rank them in order of preference)

Small land holdings ☐ Come to UK to join families/relatives ☐ To get married to the spouse settled in UK ☐ Allurement for living abroad ☐ Low income of India ☐ Heard about opportunities for prosperity in UK ☐ Unemployment at home ☐ Other ☐

3. Job-Status of Immigrants

3.1 (a) Present Job-Status

Skilled/manual work:

Factory ☐ Foundry ☐

Warehouse ☐ Building ☐

Skilled and Technical Work

Plumbers ☐ Carpenter ☐
Driver ☐ Welder ☐
Fitter ☐ Technician ☐
Electrician ☐
Professional Job: Doctors ☐
Lawyers ☐
Chartered Accountant ☐
Senior Manager ☐
University ☐
College/school Teacher ☐
Self Employed: Retail Shop ☐

(b) Job-status after arrival in UK

Unskilled/manual work:

Factory ☐ Foundry ☐

Warehouse ☐ Building ☐

Skilled and Technical Work

Plumbers ☐ Carpenter ☐
Driver ☐ Welder ☐
Fitter ☐ Technician ☐
Electrician ☐
Professional Job: Doctors ☐
Lawyers ☐
Chartered Accountant ☐
Senior Manager ☐
University ☐
College/school Teacher ☐
Self Employed: Retail Shop ☐

Skilled and Technical Work	*Skilled and Technical Work*
Small Workshop ☐ Wholesale Business ☐ Travel Agency ☐ Unemployed ☐ Not Reported ☐	Small Workshop ☐ Wholesale Business ☐ Travel Agency ☐ Unemployed ☐ Not Reported ☐

4. Foreign Remittances Sent Home

4.1 Amount of foreign remittances sent home through both official and unofficial channels since arrival in UK:

Total amount sent home since arrival in UK (Rs.)____________

Amount sent during or before 1960s (Rs.)____________

Amount sent during 1970s (Rs.)____________

Amount sent during 1980s (Rs.)____________

5. Purpose/Utilization of Foreign Remittances

5.1 State amount in rupees sent for different purposes over the period since you arrived in UK

Family maintenance____________ Construction/repairs of houses____________

Marriages, religious and social ceremonies like Akhand Path/Kirtan and death feasts etc.____________

Purchase of land____________ Agricultural improvements (like buying tractors, other farm machinery, chemicals, fertilizers, new seeds, installing tube wells/electric pumpsets and livestock, etc.)__________ Business investment (like small scale industries, setting up cooperatives, buses and loan companies, etc)__________ Bank deposits__________ Public works (like elementary school, public buildings for village weddings, and public celebrations, paving village roads and construction of temple/gurdwara, etc.__________ Other __________

5.2 Did you send money for land transaction because of

(a) to purchase land ☐ (b) to release mortgage on land ☐

5.3 What reasons made you purchase land in Punjab? To enlarge the size of land holding for prestige reasons ☐ To enlarge the size of land holding for getting sufficient income from it for living ☐ Other immigrants living in UK started buying land in Punjab ☐ Other ☐

5.4 Did you have the intention of going back to India for settlement after staying a few years in the UK? Yes ☐ No ☐

If yes, did you have the intention of going back to India for settlement even after bringing your family into UK?

Yes ☐ No ☐

5.5 When did you build pucca house in your village? Early 1960s ☐ Late 1960s ☐ Ealry 1970s☐ Late 1970s ☐ Early 1980s ☐ Late 1980s ☐

5.6 What made you build pucca house in your village? Prestige reasons ☐ Wanted to return to Punjab after staying a few years in UK ☐ For the use of your family member/relative/nearest kin ☐ Other ☐

5.7 Does any of your family members live in your pucca house? Yes ☐ No ☐

If no, who is using it? lying vacant/unoccupied ☐ Rented to school teachers/government employees at very low rent ☐ Given to government employee (free of charge) to look after the maintenance of the house ☐

5.8 Have you opened non-Resident external Account in India? Yes ☐ No ☐

5.9 Have you deposited your money in India? (a) fixed account ☐ (b) current account ☐ (c) both ☐

6. Immigrants' Awareness Regarding India's Government Schemes/Incentives for attracting Foreign Remittances

6.1 Are you fully aware of India's Government Schemes/incentives for attracting foreign remittances? Yes ☐ No ☐

If Yes, name them ______________________________

7. House Status of Immigrants

7.1 Are you living in your (a) Own house ☐ (b) Council rented house ☐ (c) Living with friends or relatives ☐

7.2 When did you buy your house? 1950s ☐ Early 1960s ☐ Late 1960s ☐ Early 1970s ☐ Late 1970s ☐ Early 1980s ☐

Late 1980s ☐

7.3 State the amount of outstanding mortgage on your house: No mortgage ☐ Less than £15000 ☐ £15000 to 30000 ☐ £30000 to 45000 ☐ More than £45000 ☐

8. Rate of various aspects of life in UK

8.1 Please state various aspects of life in UK such as:

(a) Monetary advantage: Excellent ☐ good ☐ satisfactory ☐ poor ☐ no response ☐

(b) Fair treatment at work: Excellent ☐ good ☐ satisfactory ☐ poor ☐ no response ☐

(c) Communication and transport facilities: Excellent ☐ good ☐ satisfactory ☐ poor ☐ no response ☐

(d) Clean and healthy environment: Excellent ☐ good ☐ satisfactory ☐ poor ☐ no response ☐

(e) Access to education: Excellent ☐ good ☐ satisfactory ☐ poor ☐ no response ☐

(f) Standard of living: Excellent ☐ good ☐ satisfactory ☐ poor ☐ no response ☐

(g) Self adjustment of self and family: Excellent ☐ good ☐ Satisfactory ☐ poor ☐ no response ☐

9. Assimilation Problems of Punjabi Immigrants in UK

9.1 Please rank assimilation problems in order of preference:

Cultural reasons/cultural incongruence ☐ Language problem ☐ No feeling of uniqueness ☐ Difficult to develop meaningful relations with English people ☐ Lack of involvement in public affairs ☐ Treated as second class citizen (feeling of discrimination for finding job, promotion, etc.) ☐ Mechanical/very busy life in UK ☐ Other ☐

9.2 Do you keep your ties with your family members/relatives/friends/ back home?

Strong ☐ Weak ☐ None at all ☐

10. Desire to Return or not to Return Home for Settlement

10.1 Do you want to return home for settlement? Yes ☐ No ☐

10.2 If no, give reasons for your decision not to return home for settlement (please rank them in order of preference): Adjusted well in UK ☐ No future for children in India (for unemployment, etc.) ☐ Comfortable standard of living in UK ☐ Unsafe, uncongenial, risky environment in India particularly in Punjab ☐ Hierarchical nature of organisation in India ☐ Poor transport and communication system in India ☐ Corrupt, unresponsive bureaucratic administration in India ☐ No access to good educational facilities in India ☐

The children do not want to go to India for settlement and parents want to stay with/near their children ☐ Wives do not want to go to India for settlement ☐ Other ☐

10.3 If yes, give reasons for your decision to return home for settlement (please rank them in order of preference): Strong kin and family ties in India ☐ Familiarity with environment and roots in India ☐ Cultural reasons/cultural incongruence ☐

Negative experiences encountered in UK such as racial discrimination and treatment as a second class citizen ☐ Fear of children going astray ☐ Mechanical/very busy life in UK ☐ Lonely life especially after retirement ☐ Privileged family background-wealth power, status ☐ British weather (being cold and humid) is unsuitable for aged people ☐ Other ☐

11. Education for Immigrants Children

11.1 State level of education obtained by your children: CSE ☐ Ordinarily levels ('O' levels) ☐ Advanced levels ('A' levels) ☐ Bachelor degree ☐ Master degree ☐ Apprenticeships ☐ Professional Courses (such as MBBS, Chartered Accountancy, Law Degree, MBA, etc.) ☐ No response ☐

12. The Maintenance or Non-Maintenance of Ethnic Culture by Young Sikh Girls in UK

12.1 State Yes or No for the following:

Eat beef Yes ☐ No ☐ Smoke cigarette Yes ☐ No ☐ Drink Alcohol Yes ☐ No ☐ Go to disco/parties Yes ☐ No ☐ Have boy friends Yes ☐ No ☐ Listen to English music/songs Yes ☐ No ☐ Go to temple Yes ☐ No ☐ Wear traditional dress (salwar-kameeze, etc.) Yes ☐ No ☐ Listen to Hindi songs Yes ☐ No ☐ Speak Punjabi Yes ☐ No ☐ See video of Indian films Yes ☐ No ☐

13. Immigrant's Children Views Regarding Arranged Marriage and Other Matters

13.1 Are you going to have arranged marriage? Yes ☐ No ☐

13.2 Are you expecting to have arranged marriage because of family constraints? Yes ☐ No ☐

13.3 If not for family constraints, which will you prefer? Arranged Marriage ☐ Love Marriage ☐

13.4 Have you experienced any racial discrimination in getting employment, promotion, etc.? Yes ☐ No ☐

13.5 If yes, were you short-listed for an interview in your applications? Yes ☐ No ☐

13.6 If yes, were you rejected in the majority of interviews? Yes ☐ No ☐

13.7 Do you keep ties with your relatives or someone else in India?

Strong ☐ Weak ☐ None at all ☐

BIBLIOGRAPHY

The studies referred to in the text are given in the Notes and therefore these studies are not included in this list of bibliography. The author has found the studies included in the bibliography informative and interesting and hence this bibliography may prove to be useful to those who are interested in doing research in this area.

Adams, Richard H (1991) "The Economic Uses and Impact of International Remittances in Rural Egypt", *Economic Development and Cultural Change,* Vol. 39, No. 4, July.

Addleton, J (1984) "The Impact of International Migration of Economic Development in Pakistan", *Asian Survey,* Vol. 24, No. 5, May 1984.

Aldrick, H; Carter, J; Jones, T (1986) "Asian Residential Concentration and Business Development; An analysis of shopkeepers' customers in three cities", *New Community,* Vol. XIII, No. 1, pp. 52-64.

Allen, Sheila (1971) *New Minorities, Old Conflicts — Asian and West Asian Migrants in Britain,* Toronto.

Arnold, F; Shah N (1984) "Asian Labour Migration to the Middle East", *International Migration Review,* Vol. 18, No. 2, Summer 1984.

Aurora, G S (1987) *The New Frontiersmen: A Sociological Study of Indian Immigrants in the UK,* Bombay, Popular Prakashan.

Ballard, Catherine (1978) "Arranged Marriages in British Context", *New Community,* Vol. VI, No. 3, Summer 1989, pp. 181-196.

Bald, Suresht R (1989) "The South Asian Presence in British Electoral Politics", *New Community,* Vol. 15, No. 4, July, pp. 537-548.

Baton, Michael (1972) "The Migrant Choices", *New Community,* Vol. 1, No. 5, Autumn 1972, pp. 378-382.

Bhagwati, J N (1984) "Incentives and Disincentives: International Migration *Weltwirtschaftliches Archive: Review of World Economics,* Vol. 120, No. 4, pp. 678-701.

Bhatti, F M (1976) "Language Difficulties and Social Isolation: The case of South Asian Women in Britain" *New Community,* Vol. V, Nos. 1/2, Summer 1976, pp. 115-117.

Bhattacharyya, Bharati (1985) "The Role of Family Decision in Internal Migration: The Case of India", *Journal of Development Economics,* Vol. 18, pp. 51-66.

Boneham, Margaret (1989) "Ageing and Ethnicity in Britain: The case of elderly Sikh Women in a Midland Town", *New Community,* Vol. 15, No. 3, April, pp. 447-459.

Brah, A (1978) "South Asian Teenagers in Southall: Their perceptions of marriage, family and ethnic identity", *New Community,* Vol. VI, No. 3, Summer 1978, pp. 197-206.

Brah, A (1987) "Women of South Asian Origin in Britain: Issues and Concerns", *South Asia,* Vol. 7, No. 1, pp. 39-53.

Brooks, Dennis; Singh, Karanjit (1979) "Ethnic Commitment Versus Structural Reality: South Asian Immigrant Workers in Britain", *New Community,* Vol. VII, No. 1, Winter 1978-79, pp. 19-30.

Carey, S; Shukur, A (1985) "A Profile of the Bangladesh Community in East London", *New Community,* Vol. XIII, No. 3, Winter 1985, pp. 405-419.

Central Statistical Office (Bostswana 1982) *Migration in Botswana: Pattern, Causes and Consequences—Final Report of the National Migration Study,* Gaborone, CSO, 1982, Vol. 1, 2 & 3.

Clark, P; Rughani, M (1983) "Asian Entrepreneurs in Wholesaling and Manufacturing in Leicester", *New Community,* Vol. XI, Nos. 1/2, Autumn/Winter 1983, pp. 23-33.

Chandavaskar, A B (1980) "Use of Migrants' Remittances in Labour-Exporting Countries", *Finance and Development,* Vol. 17, June 1980.

Chandrasekhar, S; ed (1982) *From India to America: A brief history of immigration: problems of discrimination, admission and assimilation,* La Jolla, California, Population Review Publications.

Cole, D A; Sambhi, P (1978) *The Sikhs, their Religion and Practices,* London: Routledge and Kegan Paul.

Desai, R H (1963) *Indian Immigrants in Britain,* London: Oxford University Press for Institute of Race Relations.

Dhanjal, B (1978) "Asian Housing in Southall: Some impressions", *New Community,* Vol. VI, Nos. 1/2, Winter 1977-78, pp. 88-93.

Fades, J (1987) *Migrants, Workers and the Social Order,* London: Tavistock.

Ghodisan, M; Essen, J (1980) "The Children of Immigrants: Social and Home Circumstances", *New Community,* Vol. VII, No. 3, Winter 1980, pp. 195-203.

Gibson, M; Bhachu, P (1986) "Community Forces and School Performance: Punjabi Sikhs In Rural California and Urban Britain", *New Community,* Vol. XIII, No. 1, Spring-Summer 1986, pp. 27-39.

Gigson, M A (1988) *Accommodation without Assimilation: Sikh Immigrants in American High School,* Cornell University Press, New York.

Gilani, T; Khan, M F; Iqbal, M (1981) *Labour Migration from Pakistan to the Middle East and its Impact on the Domestic Economy,* Research Report No. 127, Islamabad, Pakistan Institute of Development Economics, June 1981, Part 1.

Godfrey, G (ed 1986) *Migration of Asian Workers to the Arab World,* Tokyo, United Nations University, pp. 358.

Gulati, I S; Mody, Ashoka (1983) *Remittances of Indian Migrants to the Middle East: An assessment with special reference to migrants from Kerela, Working Paper No. 182,* Centre for Development Studies, Trivandrum.

Hossain, A R; Anwar, M (1984) *Remittances from International Migration: A Case Study of Bangladesh,* Manpower Planning Centre, Dhaka.

International Labour Review, ILO Publications, CH-1211 Geneva 22, Switzerland.

International Migration Review, Centre for Migration Studies, 209 Flagg Place, Staten Island, NY 10304-1199, USA.

International Migration, International Organisation for Migration, 17 Route des Morillons, Case Postale 71, 1211 Geneva 19, Switzerland.

Jackson, J A; Archer, John (1986) *Migration,* London: Longman, pp. 91.

Jacobs, Brian D (1988) *Racism in Britain,* Christopher Helm, London, pp. 205.

Jeffery, Patricia (1976) *Migrants and Refugees: Muslims and Christian Pakistani Families in Bristol,* Cambridge, Cambridge University Press.

Joseph, K V (1988) *Migration and Economic Development of Kerala,* Delhi: Mittal.

Kabra, K N (1978) *Political Economy of Brain Drain,* Arnold-Heinemann: New Delhi.

Kanitikar, H A (1972) "An Indian Elite in Britain", *New Community,* Vol. 1, No. 5, Autumn 1972, pp. 378-382.

Khandria, Binod (1990) "Migration of Human Capital to United States", *Economic and Political Weekly,* August 11, 1990, pp. 1784-1798.

Khan, V S (ed 1979) *Minorities Families in Britain,* London: Macmillan.

Khan, V S (1976) "Pakistanis in Britain: Perceptions of a population", *New Community,* Vol. 5, No. 3, pp. 222-229.

Kohler, David, F (1976) *Ethnic Minorities in Britain: Statistical Data,* 6th Edition, Community Relations Commission.

Lefebure, Allain (1990) "International Labour Migration from Two Pakistan Villages with Different Forms of Agriculture", *The Pakistan Development Review,* Vol. 29, No. 1, pp. 59-90.

Lipshitz, Gabriel (1991) "Immigration and International Migration as a Mechanism of Polarization and Dispersion of Population and Development: The case of Israel", *Economic Development and Cultural Change,* Vol. 39, No. 2, pp. 391-408.

Lipton, Michael (1980) "Migration from Rural Areas of Poor Countries: The Impact on Rural Productivity and Income Distribution", *World Development,* Vol. 8, January 1980:12.

Lomas, G B (1973) Census 1971 - *The Cloured Population of Great Britain: A comparative study of coloured households in four country boroughs,* London, Runnymede Trust.

Macmillan, M J "The Economic Effects of International Migration: A survey" *Journal of Common Market Studies,* Vol. 20, No. 3, March 1982.

Mahmood, Raisal Awal (1988) "Overseas Remittances and the Bangladesh Economy", *Bangladesh Journal of Political Economy,* Vol. 8, No. 2, pp. 159-181.

Mahmood, Raisal Awal (1980) *Emigrants' Remittances as a Source of Foreign Exchange—The Experience of Bangladesh,* IDS, Sussex University, UK, Mimeo, 1980.

Mayer, Martin N (1989) "Asians in Northern Ireland Economy", *New Community,* Vol. 15, No. 2, January, pp. 203-210.

McEvoy, D; Paul, V; Furnham, A (1986) "Some Explanations for Immigration to, and Emigration from, Britain", *New Community,* Vol. XIII, No. 1, pp. 65-78.

McGrath, M (1976) "The Economic Position of Asian Immigrants in Batley", *New Community,* Vol. V, No. 3, Autumn 1976, pp. 239-249.

Mercer, John (1989) "Asian Migrants and Residential Location in Canada", *New Community,* Vol. 15, No. 2, January, pp. 185-202.

Mowli, Chandra V (1982) *Bridging the Gulf — India's Manpower Migration to West Asia,* New Delhi, Sterling.

Nair, Gopinathan P.R. (1988) *Incidence, Impact and Implications of Migration Migration to the Middle East from Kerala,* Trivandrum, Mimeo.

Nayyar, D (1987) *International Labour Migration from India: A Micro-Economic Analysis, Working Paper No. 3,* ILO, UNDP, RAS/85/009, New Delhi.

Nayyar Deepak (1994) *Migration, Remittances and Capital Flows — The Indian Experience,* Delhi: Oxford University.

Organisation for Economic Cooperation and Development (1979) *Migration Growth and Development,* Paris, OECD, pp. 59.

Parekh, Bikhu (ed.) (1974) *Colour, Culture and Consciousness: Immigrant Intellectuals in Britain,* London, 1974.

Pettigrew, Joyce (1972) "Some Observations on the Social System of the Sikh Jats", *New Community,* Vol. 1, No. 5, Autumn 1972, pp. 354-363.

Pocock, D F (1976) "Preservation of the Religious Life: Hindu Immigrants in England" *Contributions to Indian Sociology,* Vol. 10, No. 2, pp. 341-365.

Price, C (1969) "A Study of Assimilation", in Jackson, J A; Migration, Cambridge, 1969.

Rex, John; Moose, R (1967) *Race, Community and Conflict,* London, 1967.

Richmond, Anthony (1975) "Black and Asian Immigrants in Britain and Canada", *New Community,* Vol. IV, No. 4, Winter/Spring 1976, pp. 507-516.

Robinson, V; Flintoff Ian (1982) "Asian Retailing in Coventry", *New Community,* Vol. X, No. 2, Winter 1982, pp. 251-258.

Robinson, V (1988) "The New Indian Middle Class in Britain", *Ethnic and Racial Studies,* Vol. 11, No. 4, pp. 456-473.

Sheth, N R (1968) *The Social Framework of an Indian Factory,* Manchester: Manchester University Press, 1968.

Sills, A; Tarpey, M; Golding, P "Asians in an Inner City", *New Community,* Vol. XI, Nos. 1/2, Autumn/Winter 1983, pp. 34-41.

Singh, Khuswant (1963) *A History of the Sikhs,* London: Oxford University Press.

Socknat, James A (1978) *Migration for Employment Abroad and Its Impact on Development in the Yemen Arab Republic:* International Migration Project: Durham University, 1978.

Stark, Odded (1980 "On the Role of Urban to Rural Remittances in Rural Development", *Journal of Development Studies,* Vol. 16, No. 3, April 1980.

Stark, Odded; Lucas, Robert E B "Migration Remittances and the Family", *Economic Development and Cultural Change,* Vol. 36, No. 3, April 1988, pp. 465-481.

Stahl, Charles W (1989) "The Impact of Overseas Workers' Remittances on Indigenous Industries: Evidence from Bangladesh", *The Developing Economies,* Vol. 27, No. 3, September 1989, pp. 269-285.

Stahl, C W; Arnold, F (1986) "Overseas Workers' Remittances in Asian Development", *International Migration Review,* Special Issue: Remittances, Winter 1986.

Wallman, S (1979) *Ethnicity at Work,* London Macmillan.

World Bank (1981) *Labour Migration from Bangladesh to Middle East.* Staff Working Paper, No. 454, Washington DC, April 1981.

World Bank (1981) *International Migrant Workers' Remittances: Issues and Prospects,* Staff Working Paper No. 481, August 1981.

INDEX